MARTIN LUTHER KING, JR. DAY

REVISED AND UPDATED

Dianne M. MacMillan

Enslow Elementary
an imprint of
Enslow Publishers, Inc.
40 Industrial Road
Box 398
Berkeley Heights, NJ 07922
USA
http://www.enslow.com

Enslow Elementary, an imprint of Enslow Publishers, Inc.

Enslow Elementary® is a registered trademark of Enslow Publishers, Inc.

Library of Congress CataloginginPublication Data

MacMillan, Dianne M., 1943-
　　Martin Luther King, Jr. Day / Dianne M. MacMillan. — 2nd ed.
　　　　p. cm. — (Best holiday books)
　　Includes bibliographical references and index.
　　Audience: Grades K-3.
　　ISBN-13: 978-0-7660-3043-5
　　ISBN-10: 0-7660-3043-1
　　1. Martin Luther King, Jr., Day—Juvenile literature. 2. King, Martin Luther, Jr.,
1929–1968—Juvenile literature. 3. African Americans—Biography—Juvenile literature.
4. Baptists—United States—Clergy—Biography—Juvenile literature. 5. Civil rights
workers—United States—Biography—Juvenile literature. I. Title.
　　E185.97.K5M25 2008
　　394.261—dc22
　　　　　　　　　　　　　　　　2007002423

Printed in the United States of America

10 9 8 7 6 5 4 3 2 1

To Our Readers: We have done our best to make sure all Internet Addresses in this book were active and appropriate when we went to press. However, the author and the publisher have no control over and assume no liability for the material available on those Internet sites or on other Web sites they may link to. Any comments or suggestions can be sent by e-mail to comments@enslow.com or to the address on the back cover.

Every effort has been made to locate all copyright holders of material used in this book. If any errors or omissions have occurred, corrections will be made in future editions of this book.

Cover Photograph: Associated Press

Photo Credits: Alabama Department of Archives and History, p. 32; AP, pp. 1, 3, 4, 6, 12, 17, 19 (left), 23 (bottom), 24, 27, 29, 35, 42, 44; Courtesy New England Conservatory, p. 14; Courtesy Ronald Reagan Library, p. 37; David Phillips, p. 8; John Goodwyn, Montgomery, Alabama, p. 16; © District of Columbia Public Library, p. 39; Donnie and Connie Shackleford, p. 19 (right); LBJ Library photo by Yoichi R. Okamoto, p. 33; Library of Congress, pp. 9, 13, 23 (top); Stephanie Cassamas, p. 40 (bottom); Wally Gobetz, p. 40 (top).

Contents

Dr. Martin Luther King, Jr. won the Nobel Peace Prize in 1964 for his efforts to create equality in the United States.

A MAN WHO CHANGED HISTORY

JANUARY 20, 1986, was an important day. It was the first Martin Luther King, Jr. Day.

Martin Luther King, Jr. believed everyone should be free to make his or her own choices. They should be free to work at any job, or attend any school. Everyone should be able to do the same things.

At one time, many laws in our country were unfair to African Americans. Martin Luther King, Jr., spent his life fighting to change those laws. He did not fight with weapons. Instead, he fought with words and ideas. He helped change the history of our country.

Many people, both young and old, march in parades on Martin Luther King, Jr. Day.

KING'S EARLY YEARS

MARTIN LUTHER KING, JR., was born on January 15, 1929. He lived in Atlanta, Georgia. His parents called him M.L. His sister, Willie Christine, was one year older. His younger brother, Alfred Daniel, was called A.D. Martin's father was the minister of the Ebenezer Baptist Church. Everyone called Martin's father Daddy King. Martin's mother, Alberta, played the organ and sang in church.

Martin Luther King, Jr.'s childhood home in Atlanta, Georgia.

The church was a big part of Martin's early life. On Sundays, he listened to his father speak. Martin loved big words. He saw how words could make people feel happy or sad. He told his mother that some day he was going to use big words like that.

Martin's best friends lived across the street. They played together every day. But one day the boys' mother told Martin to go home. She said her sons could never play with him again. Martin asked her why. She said it was because her sons were white. Martin was black. Martin went home crying.

Martin's mother tried to explain. She said that black people were brought to

This man is drinking water from a segregated fountain at an Oklahoma streetcar station in 1939.

America from Africa long ago. They were brought to work in the fields as slaves.

After the Civil War was fought in our country in the 1860s, the slaves were set free. But many white people still did not want to let black people be free. White people made unfair laws. One law said that black children and white children could not go to the same school. Another said that black people could not eat in restaurants where white people ate. There were parks, bathrooms, and drinking fountains that had signs that said Whites Only.

Martin's mother said these laws kept black people and white people apart, or separate. Keeping people apart because of race is called segregation. But then she said to Martin, "You are as good as anyone."

MARTIN BECOMES A YOUNG MAN

MARTIN LOVED BOOKS. He learned to read before he started school. He also enjoyed all kinds of sports. Even though he was small, he played hard. Everyone wanted him on their baseball or football teams.

Martin was a good speaker. In high school, he won prizes for his speeches. Once, Martin gave a speech in another town. It was a long bus trip. Buses were segregated.

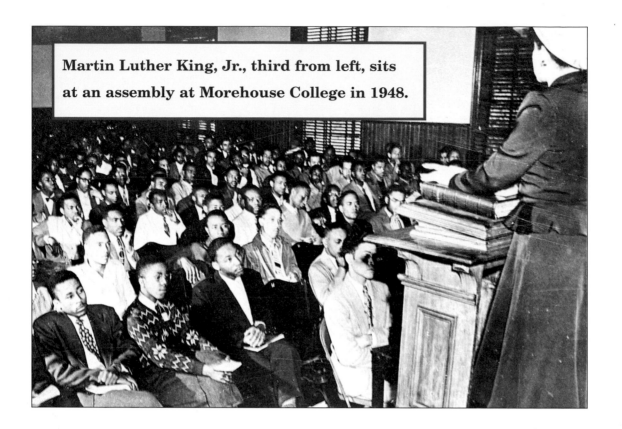

Martin Luther King, Jr., third from left, sits at an assembly at Morehouse College in 1948.

Black people could not sit near white people. They had to sit in the back rows. White people sat in the front rows. But when the seats for white people became filled, black people had to give them their seats.

After Martin gave his speech, he and his teacher left for home. They sat down on the bus. White people got on. The bus driver told Martin to give up his seat. Martin refused. The bus driver became angry. He called Martin names. He said he would call the police. Martin's teacher asked Martin to obey the law. Martin and his teacher stood for the ninety-mile trip.

Martin skipped both ninth and twelfth grade. When he was fifteen, he entered Morehouse College. He decided to become a minister like his father.

After Morehouse, Martin went to Crozer Theological Seminary in Pennsylvania. He made many friends. He graduated as the best student in his class. Martin won money to study at Boston University.

Martin studied the ideas and lives of many great men. He read about Jesus, Frederick Douglass, and Henry David Thoreau. Then Martin studied the life of Mahatma Gandhi.

Dr. King was inspired by Gandhi's ideas. Here, Gandhi is spinning thread to make clothes.

Martin Luther King, Jr. married Coretta Scott in 1953.

Gandhi lived in India in the 1940s. Gandhi fought without weapons for freedom. He did this by refusing to obey unfair laws. Even when put in jail, he would not give in. Gandhi never used strong force or violence. Gandhi called this "nonviolent resistance."

While studying at Boston University, Martin met a girl named Coretta Scott. She was studying music. They were both from the South. They liked books, music, and talking about ideas. Soon they fell in love. In 1953, they were married by Martin's father at Coretta's home in Alabama.

DEXTER AVENUE BAPTIST CHURCH

IN 1954, King became pastor of the Dexter Avenue Baptist Church in Montgomery, Alabama. In 1955, after receiving his degree from Boston University, Martin was called Dr. King.

Soon the Kings' first child was born. They named her Yolanda but called her Yoki. Coretta and Martin were very happy. But their lives changed on December 1, 1955.

Martin Luther King, Jr. became the pastor of the Dexter Avenue Baptist Church in Montgomery, Alabama, in 1954.

On that day, a black woman named Rosa Parks did a brave thing.

Rosa Parks worked in a Montgomery store. At night, she was very tired. On Thursday, December 1, 1955, she climbed on the bus and sank into her seat. The bus made more stops. More white people got on. The bus driver told Rosa to stand. Rosa refused. She was tired, and it was not fair. The bus driver called the police. Rosa was taken to jail.

By Friday, everyone in the black neighborhood knew about Rosa. They were angry at the police and at the bus company. They wanted the bus company to make changes. Martin and other leaders decided to ask all black people to stop riding the buses. This is called a boycott.

Notices were printed and passed out. They said: "Don't ride the bus to work, to town, to school, or to any place Monday, December 5." The notice also said to come to a meeting on Monday night.

No one knew if this plan would work. On Monday morning, Coretta and Martin King looked out their window. A bus

Rosa Parks inspired Martin Luther King, Jr. to fight segregation.

went by. It was empty. Then another rolled by. It was also empty. The Kings were excited.

All day long, people walked when they had to go someplace. Some had to walk as far as fourteen miles to get to their jobs. That night, more than four thousand people came to the meeting. Dr. King spoke. This was the first time most of them had heard him speak. Dr. King said, "There comes a time when people get tired. We are here this evening to say we are tired of being segregated . . . " Everyone cheered. They voted to continue the boycott until the bus company made changes.

A group was formed to lead the boycott. Dr. King was elected president.

Day after day, people stayed away from the buses. Some days it rained and the weather was cold. Black people walked. Some rode horses. Others shared rides. The buses remained empty. Black people were doing a brave and dangerous thing.

Dr. King spoke all over Montgomery. He asked people to stay away from the buses.

One night, while giving a speech, Dr. King's house was bombed. Quickly, he rushed home. He found Coretta and Yoki

Martin Luther King, Jr.'s home (below) was bombed on January 30, 1956. Windows were broken, but no one was hurt. King spoke to the crowd that gathered afterwards (left), urging them to stay calm.

safe. But the front of his house had been destroyed. The police were there. The yard was filled with friends and neighbors. They were angry at the people who bombed Dr. King's house. They had sticks and broken bottles. They were ready to fight the police.

Dr. King told the crowd, "If you have weapons, take them home. We must love our white brothers. We must meet hate with love."

He was telling them what he had learned from Jesus, and Gandhi. He was speaking about nonviolence. The crowd went home. No one was hurt.

Finally, the U.S. Supreme Court, the highest court in our country, said that segregation on city buses was wrong. The bus company changed its rules. Black people could sit anywhere on the bus. They no longer had to give up their seats.

A NEW GROUP

AFTER THE MONTGOMERY BOYCOTT, Dr. King and other black ministers began the Southern Christian Leadership Conference (SCLC). The aim of this group was to change unfair laws. Dr. King went all over the United States. He told everyone how to fight unfair laws. He said they must be peaceful. If the police took them to jail, they should go quietly. Even if people hurt them, they must not hurt others.

People marched down streets carrying signs about unfair laws. As more people heard Dr. King speak, more people tried his ideas. Black college students sat peacefully at white lunch counters. Black people went to white parks. They used bathrooms and drinking fountains that had Whites Only signs. Many black people were put in jail. Some were beaten and even killed. Dr. King himself was taken to jail many times.

The Kings now had four children—Yolanda, Martin III, Dexter, and Bernice. They would ask why Daddy was in jail. Their mother would say, "Daddy is helping people."

One Sunday, Dr. King told the people of the Dexter Avenue Baptist Church that he had to leave. He was moving away from Montgomery. He needed to spend more time with the SCLC. Its office was in Atlanta. The people were very sad. They all joined hands and sang a hymn. Dr. King looked around the room full of friends and cried.

Dr. King and many others held sit-ins and demonstrations to change unfair laws. Above, protesters sit at a lunch counter that was reserved for white people only.

To the left, Dr. King is welcomed home from jail by his wife, two of his children, and several friends and supporters.

Dr. King and Coretta Scott King pose in their Atlanta home in 1963 with Martin Luther King, III (left), Dexter Scott, and Yolanda (right).

"I HAVE A DREAM"

MARTIN AND CORETTA KING moved their family to Atlanta. Dr. King was away a great deal of the time. But when he was home, it was a happy time. His wife, Coretta, would cook some of his favorite foods. He liked pork chops, fried chicken, black-eyed peas, and greens.

The children loved playing with their father. He would tickle and tease them. A favorite game was to climb halfway up the stairs. Then they would jump into their

Water was turned on the children. Then they were attacked. The police arrested 959 boys and girls.

That night people all over the country watched the news. They saw the children. They saw what happened. Many were angry and upset. Finally the men who ran the city met with the black leaders. They ended the unfair laws. Freedom for African Americans had come to Birmingham!

On August 28, 1963, Martin Luther King, Jr., and other black leaders marched into Washington, D.C. They were followed by two hundred fifty thousand people. Most of the people were black. But there were also thousands of white people. They wanted to join Dr. King's fight for freedom.

The crowd gathered in front of the Lincoln Memorial. There were songs and speeches. Then Dr. Martin Luther King, Jr. prepared to speak.

On August 28, 1963, Martin Luther King, Jr. waved to the crowd from the steps of the Lincoln Memorial in Washington, D.C., where he gave his famous "I Have a Dream" speech.

Dr. King said, "I have a dream today!" And then he told of his dream:

I have a dream that one day on the red hills of Georgia the sons of former slaves and the sons of former slave owners will be able to sit down together at the table of brotherhood…

I have a dream that my four little children will one day live in a nation where they will not be judged by the color of their skin, but by the content of their character.

He dreamed of freedom ringing from every mountain. He dreamed of all God's children joining hands. He dreamed of all men singing together, "We are free at last."

When Dr. King had finished speaking, people cheered. Many were crying. Then, everyone joined hands and sang together, "We Shall Overcome."

THE NOBEL PEACE PRIZE

EACH YEAR the country of Norway gives a prize. The prize goes to the person who had done the most for peace in the world for that year. It is called the Nobel Peace Prize. In October 1964, Martin Luther King, Jr. was told that he had won. He was then thirty-five years old. He was the youngest man and the second African American to win the honor. In December, he and his wife went to Norway to accept the prize.

In 1965, Dr. King (near front, beneath arrow) led a march in Alabama from Selma to Montgomery so that everyone in the state would be allowed to vote.

After the Kings returned home, Dr. King continued his fight. Before a person can vote, his or her name has to be on a list or register. Most black people in the South could not get their names on the list. There were many unfair rules.

Dr. King tried to get black people on the list in Alabama. The state leaders wouldn't allow it. Dr. King planned a fifty-four mile march. The march would start in Selma, Alabama. It would end at the state capitol building in Montgomery.

On March 6, 1965, the march began. Many white people from the North joined the Selma march. Some marchers were beaten and put into jail. Some were killed. President Lyndon Johnson ordered soldiers to protect them. Finally, three hundred people reached Montgomery. Partly because of the Selma march, President Johnson asked Congress to pass a voting rights bill. In August 1965, the law was passed. Millions of black people could vote at last.

Dr. King and President Lyndon B. Johnson meet in the Oval Office at the White House.

DR. KING'S DEATH

NOW DR. KING turned his attention to help poor people. He held marches in Chicago, Illinois, for better housing. He planned a Poor People's March for Washington, D.C. In April 1968, he flew to Memphis, Tennessee, to help the garbage workers get equal pay.

At 6:40 P.M. on April 4, Dr. King stepped out of his hotel room. From across the street, James Earl Ray fired a shot. Dr. King fell. An hour later, he was dead. Dr. Martin

Luther King, Jr., was only thirty-nine years old. The world was in shock.

Dr. King was buried in Atlanta. An old farm wagon carried his body. It was pulled by two mules. Behind the wagon walked one hundred thousand people—rich and poor, known and unknown, black and white. On his grave are printed the words that he used to end many of his speeches: "Free at last. Free at last. Thank God Almighty, I'm free at last."

Many people marched at Dr. King's funeral. His family and close friends walk in front, with Coretta in the center.

A NEW HOLIDAY

AFTER DR. KING'S DEATH, many people wanted to have a holiday to honor him. It had to be voted on by Congress. Every year the idea was presented. Each time there were not enough votes. But Coretta Scott King and others never gave up hope. They spoke to leaders in government. Thousands of people wrote letters. African Americans in all fifty states asked their state leaders for a holiday.

On January 15, 1981, one hundred thousand people marched in Washington, D.C. They wanted to show how important the holiday was to them.

Finally, fifteen years after Dr. King's death, Congress voted for the holiday. On November 2, 1983, President Ronald Reagan signed the law. The third Monday of January would become Martin Luther King, Jr. Day.

Coretta Scott King (left) watches as President Reagan signs a law in 1983 creating a national Martin Luther King, Jr. holiday.

DR. KING IS REMEMBERED

A YEAR AFTER Dr. King's death, Coretta Scott King formed the Martin Luther King, Jr. Center for Nonviolent Social Change. The center is in Atlanta. It is a way of remembering Dr. King. Dr. King is buried there. At the center, people learn about nonviolence. They come from all over the world. They read Dr. King's papers. They are taught how to use peaceful ways to change unfair laws.

Dr. King is remembered in many other ways, too. All across the country, schools, libraries, parks, and streets are named after him. In Los Angeles, there is a Martin Luther King, Jr. Hospital. The Dr. Martin Luther King Bridge crosses

This mural shows Dr. King in a cap and gown while Gandhi and others watch over him.

the Mississippi River in St. Louis. The Martin Luther King Memorial Library is in Washington, D.C. In Memphis, there is a park named for him. In the country of Israel, a forest was planted to honor him. And around the world there have been more than 105 different postage stamps in his honor.

The statue of doves above is a tribute to Dr. King. Doves represent peace. The memorial to the right shows where Dr. King and Coretta are buried at The King Center in Atlanta.

REV. MARTIN LUTHER KING, JR.
1929 – 1968
"Free at last, Free at last,
Thank God Almighty
I'm Free at last."

CORETTA SCOTT KING
1927 – 2006
"And now abide Faith, Hope,
Love, These Three; but the
greatest of these is Love."
1 Cor. 13:13

PREPARING FOR THE HOLIDAY

EVERY JANUARY, children prepare for Martin Luther King, Jr. Day. They read books about Dr. King. They learn about his childhood. They talk about segregation. Boys and girls draw pictures of Dr. King. They put on plays about his life.

Children talk about how to settle fights peacefully. They ask themselves, "What would Dr. King do? What would he say?" Everyone shares ideas about love instead of hate.

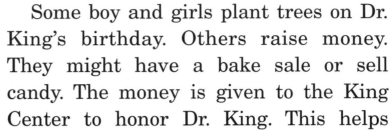
This girl colors a picture of Dr. King as she learns about him at school.

Some boy and girls plant trees on Dr. King's birthday. Others raise money. They might have a bake sale or sell candy. The money is given to the King Center to honor Dr. King. This helps the King Center spread Dr. King's ideas.

Films about Dr. King's life are shown. Reports are given about Dr. King's speeches. People talk about how Dr. King fought to help poor people. Children bring food and clothes to school. These are given to poor people in their neighborhood.

Everywhere, children talk about the unfair laws that Dr. King helped change. They learn why we honor this man.

THE THIRD MONDAY IN JANUARY

MARTIN LUTHER KING, JR. DAY is a national holiday. On that day, mail is not delivered. All U.S. government offices and most banks are closed. Many schools and businesses are closed. Parades are held in cities all over our country. In churches, people pray for freedom. They pray that people everywhere will have fair laws.

In Atlanta and Montgomery, people visit the places where Dr. King worked and lived. Leaders of the SCLC and African-American groups give speeches about Dr. King and his dreams.

Martin Luther King, Jr., died before his dreams could come true. But his dreams live on. His words still speak to us. And on this holiday, we can remember the man who changed our country and our world.

Dr. Martin Luther King, Jr.'s words continue to inspire people all over the world.

GLOSSARY

boycott—To join with others in refusing to deal with a person, business, or government

capitol—A building where laws are made for a nation or state.

Civil War—The war in the United States between the Northern states and the Southern states from 1861 to 1865.

Congress—A branch of government that makes laws.

Nobel Peace Prize—A prize given each year by the country of Norway to the person who has done the most that year for peace.

nonviolent—Not violent; peaceful.

resistance—The effort of fighting against or overcoming.

segregation—The setting apart of one racial group from another racial group.

Southern Christian Leadership Conference (SCLC)—A group formed to fight unfair laws.

Supreme Court—The highest court in the United States.

violence—Acts that hurt or destroy people, places or things.

Further Reading

Marx, David F. *Martin Luther King, Jr. Day*. New York: Children's Press, 2001.

Murray, Julie. *Martin Luther King, Jr. Day*. Edina, Minn.: Abdo Pub., 2005.

Nelson, Robin. *Martin Luther King, Jr. Day*. Minneapolis: Lerner Publications Co., 2003.

Internet Addresses

The King Center
http://www.thekingcenter.org/

Martin Luther King, Jr. Day
http://www.kidsdomain.com/holiday/mlk/index.html

Martin Luther King, Jr. Day
Activities and Resources for Kids
http://fun.familyeducation.com/martin-luther-king-jr/activities/32832.html

INDEX